WISDOM
for Everyday Living

by AYANA BERNARD

WISDOM *for Everyday Living*

Copyright © 2017 by Ayana Bernard

All Rights Reserved. No part of this book may be reproduced or transmitted in any form or by any means, electronically or mechanically, including photocopying, recording or by an information storage and retrieval system without permission in writing from the author of this book.

Scriptures taken from the Holy Bible, New International Version®, NIV®. Copyright © 1973, 1978, 1984, 2011 by Biblica, Inc.™ Used by permission of Zondervan. All rights reserved worldwide. www.zondervan.com The "NIV" and "New International Version" are trademarks registered in the United States Patent and Trademark Office by Biblica, Inc.™

Scripture taken from the New King James Version®. Copyright © 1982 by Thomas Nelson. Used by permission. All rights reserved.

ISBN: 978-0-692-84318-5

Library of Congress In Publication Data

Author: Ayana Bernard | YanniAyana1@gmail.com

Editors: Dr. Ruth Baskerville &
Mauva Maria Morrison

Photographer: Michael Cairns | Wet Orange Studio | Orlando

Book Designer: Eli Blyden | EliTheBookGuy.com

Printed in the United States of America

Dedications

*To my parents,
Michael Bernard and Maria Morrison*

Wisdom For Everyday Living

Acknowledgements

I thank GOD for giving me the grace to complete this book, "WISDOM For Everyday Living."

~

I would also like to give a special thank you to Mauva Maria Morrison

Wisdom For Everyday Living

Contents

Dedications iii

Acknowledgements v

Introductions 1

Your Focus! 3

You Can Heal! 5

I Am Always With You! 7

The Packed Schedule 9

A New Mind 11

I Am Proud Of You! 13

The Swap 15

Don't Go Back! 17

A Time Of Training! 19

Value God's Word! 21

Did Your Best? Now Rest! 23

Don't Make It Happen! Just Be! 25

Your Gifts & Talents Needs An Outlet! ... 28

Unexpected Opportunities! 30

Peter, Do You Love Me!	32
The Good Part!	34
Transformation Through Pain	36
Troubled About Many Things!	38
It's What's Right With You!	40
Be Slow To React!	42
In Christ, You Never Lose!	44
Forgiveness & Trust	46
Read God's Word	48
A Soft Answer	50
Stay Thankful	52
Don't Worry	54
Affirmations	56
Overcome Evil with Good	58
Give Him You!	61
Emotions	63
Courage Is A Gift	65
Remove The Mountain	68
It's Personal!	70

Use The Name! 72

The Spirit Check! 74

Release The Grip! 76

Intentionally Cruel 78

Validation.. 80

Freedom Has A Purpose 83

God Promotes! 85

Action Needed 87

On Your Mind... 89

Keep Your Eyes On Him 91

Building Blocks 94

Conclusion 96

You Are Needed 98

Learn From Feedback 100

Just Ask... 102

Rest 104

You Are A Champion 106

Wisdom For Everyday Living

Introductions

Dear Special One,

The wisdom nuggets in this book are brief summaries of the many lessons I've learned in my own life! I am a person who thirsts for wisdom and inspiration. In writing this book, I wanted to provide this combination for those who desire to experience more victory in their walk with God.

God gives wisdom to those who ask in faith. He provides us with inspiration to remind us of His love, and to encourage us to stay positive on our journey with Him. It is my prayer that this book blesses you tremendously, and causes you to think, live, and learn.

Enjoy "Wisdom For Everyday Living!"

Love,
Yanni

Wisdom For Everyday Living

Your Focus!

What is it on, your problems, negativity, the past?

Past victories, past failures, or perhaps all of the people who did you wrong?

Are you focused

On your finances, or on everything you do not have in your life?

SHIFT YOUR FOCUS!

God has given you the power IN HIM to control your thoughts.

Be careful what you gaze upon! Whatever you FOCUS on becomes BIG to YOU!

Your attention gives it greatness, and power!

REDIRECT YOUR FOCUS ON JESUS!

The Author & Finisher of your faith! Meditate, and know God's word.

Remember the wonderful promises you have IN HIM!

Remember His faithfulness towards you!

Meditating on God's goodness, mercy, and grace will keep you in perfect peace. Isaiah 26:3 (KJV), *"Thou wilt keep him in perfect peace, whose mind is stayed on thee: because he trusteth in thee."*

Exalt God in your life!

Then you will see your problems & circumstances as they really are, and you'll put them in their proper place!

They are not bigger than your God! Your problems are under His feet, in His Sovereign control!

When you change your focus to Christ, you change your focus to VICTORY!

You Can Heal!

Yes, it is possible.

As long as you have life, it is God's desire for you to be completely whole.

Your past sufferings doesn't have to control you!

It doesn't have to be a stumbling block in your now, or in your future!

But you ask, "How can it not be a stumbling block? The pain is real! It affects my daily life! The damage! The hurt! You don't have a clue!

There are memories, words that replay in my mind, and tears that blind my eyes.

The shakes, trembles of anxiety, torments of fear, my thoughts, the regret, the rage! My emotions are in a whirlwind!"

And I say, "YOU CAN HEAL!"

This doesn't have to be the conclusion of your life.

YES! I say this through Jesus Christ, to stir your hope to believe again. For the Bible says, *"...By His stripes we are healed."* Isaiah 53:5 (NKJV)

Jesus is the only ONE who will heal you, layer by layer. HE will destroy the root, remove the residue, and fill that area with HIS very presence. Peace, a future, joy, love, courage, laughter will be yours again!

Jeremiah 29:11 (NIV) says, *"plans to prosper you and not to harm you..."*

God has a plan for you! A life better than you can pray for yourself, regardless, of its many challenges. His love for you is perfect, and will eliminate all shame.

Have faith in God! Trust in Him! Get your hopes up, because YOU CAN HEAL!

I Am Always with You!

I heard these words in my heart from the Lord! It is a reminder that is necessary to keep you in a state of calm & peace.

It is protection from anxiety about all of the things you can't control.

Remember this! Whatever arises, God allowed it and has equipped you with the power to handle it!

The greatest comfort is that God lives in you! He is not afar off!

Your body is His temple, His home. He looks through your eyes, feels what you feel, touch what you touch!

You are His vessel, the place where His Spirit dwells.

God is able to meet your every need!

His omnipresence makes Him everywhere at the same time! God is not limited! You always have His attention!

God is always with you! This truth is where your confidence lies! Remember,

Philippians 4:13 (NKJV), *"I can do all things through Christ who strengthens me."*

Fortify your confidence in Isaiah 41:10 (NKJV), where God says, *"I will strengthen you, Yes, I will help you, I will uphold you with My righteous right hand."* Have faith in Christ's Love for you! He says to you, *"Fear Not. I Love You."*

I AM ALWAYS WITH YOU!

The Packed Schedule

There is always something going on!

You feel the pressure from those you care about, wanting to show your support for every invite you receive! How do you decide what not to do?

Do you ever say, "No?" Is there a fear of missing out? You know, the torment of wondering what will happen, and what you will miss if you're not there.

We all like to know what's going on! God had to show me that a lot of the decisions I made were rooted in my fear of missing out on what could happen! I had the fear of being a disappointment to others, and not meeting expectations. Fear and anxiety made me a people-pleaser, which led to a very stressful, overly packed schedule! God had to teach me when to say, "NO" and have peace with my "NO!"

In different seasons in my life, I have had to release my commitment from group activities I have been involved in for years. Of course, there were some peers who did not understand. There were times I didn't completely understand my decisions. However, when we believe we are being led by God, we have to be obedient and settle on the decision inside of us. Always know that when you walk in obedience to God, all will eventually go well for you, and for others connected to you, because you are in His will.

When invitations arise, my prayer now is, "Lord, do I need to attend this event?" Proverbs 3:5-6 (KJV) says, *"Trust in the Lord with all thine heart; and lean not unto thine own understanding. In all thy ways acknowledge him, and he shall direct thy paths."*

Reduce the stress! Examine the PACKED SCHEDULE

A New Mind

Your MIND is incredible! It can be renewed! You have the ability to add or remove information. Christ has given us the power to control thoughts that try to take residence in our minds.

2Corinthians 10:5 (KJV) tells us how to handle ill-thoughts that enter our minds: *"Casting down imaginations, and every high thing that exalteth itself against the knowledge of God, and bringing into captivity every thought to the obedience of Christ."* Pay attention to your thoughts. Align your faith with God's Word.

Come into agreement with what God says about you. No longer entertain or agree with negative thoughts about yourself. You are wonderfully made, and have limitless ability in Christ Jesus! Feed yourself the Word of God daily, to obtain a new mindset.

Romans 12:2 (NIV) tells us, *"Do not conform to the pattern of this world, but be transformed by the renewing of your mind."* Your attitude, emotions, and well-being, will change as you renew your mind with the Word of God.

Take this challenge: Examine your thoughts and replace negative ones with scriptures from God's word. For example, if your thoughts suggest God is angry with you- use your faith and say, "I cast down that thought! I am forgiven! I put on Christ's righteousness! I am the apple of God's eye!" Shut the negative thoughts down & replace them with good! You will enjoy a better life, with a

NEW MIND.

I Am Proud Of You!

So frustrated with the same temptation coming to me over and over again!

Tired of resisting, I gave in and I did it! Then in the act I realized, this is stupid!! What am I doing? I don't even enjoy it! So I stopped and repented to the Lord!

"Lord, sorry that I fell! Sorry, I just caved and gave in because I was tired of resisting the same temptation day and night!" The Lord said to me, *"Don't be dismayed! Don't get discouraged! I AM PROUD OF YOU! Look at you! Look at how much you have changed!"*

I was confused, baffled about what I heard in my spirit. I was resisting feelings of guilt and condemnation by repeating 1John 1:9 (KJV), *"If we confess our sins, he is faithful and just to forgive us our sins, and to cleanse us from all unrighteousness."*

Then I said to the Lord, "You're proud of me?!" He said, *"YES! Think of your*

spiritual daughter, whom you have corrected about an act. You watch her do it again, but this time, by her own choice she stops in the middle of the act, corrects herself and doesn't do it anymore. Wouldn't you be proud of her?" I said, "YES, because I would see how much she has matured."

The Lord then said to me, *"That is why I am proud of you! Don't focus on your mistakes. Focus on how much you have changed through your relationship with me. Receive my mercy. Forgive yourself. Have faith in my unconditional love for you!*

Get up! Let's continue! Be assured!

I AM PROUD OF YOU!"

The Swap

Every thought or image that comes into your mind is not yours. All the enemy can do to you is make suggestions. He continuously tries to plant thoughts

in your mind to get you to meditate on them, and take wrong actions.

We have the responsibility of examining our thoughts. We have to pay attention to the words, ideas, images that come into our minds. 2Corinthians 10:5 (KJV) says for us to take captive every thought, to make it obedient to Christ! Do you know what we have to do? We have to do the SWAP!

We exchange one thought for another! We identify the dark thoughts and images, and replace them with the Word of God!

We have to read and meditate on God's Word! It is our strength, our confidence, our faith, and our ability to walk in Victory daily!

When crazy, dark thoughts, bad conversations, negative words about yourself, or others come to your mind, do the SWAP!

Plead the Blood of Jesus over your mind, declare Philippians 4:8 (KJV), and think on things that are holy, pure, of virtue, and good report. Declare to yourself that you have the mind of Christ!

The SWAP is a continuous practice, and will bring you into victory! No longer tolerate any old thought that enters your mind. Take hold of it, and replace it with positive declarations. We overcome evil with good!

DO THE SWAP!

Don't Go Back!

Isn't it strange? When you're separated from a toxic relationship for awhile, you recall mostly good memories.

This is a deception because you don't remember the reasons why it became necessary for you to separate. You remember the good times and less of the bad. God has delivered you from the situation, and your emotions want you to get back entangled with it.

When you are vulnerable and alone, it is easy to meditate on the good and entertain the possibility of things being better if you return. However, you must decide in your heart to not go back to what God has intentionally delivered you from. It was toxic, it was destructive, and God is still restoring you from the damage from those negative connections. Look how far you have come! You're not the same person you used to be! Look at your maturity in Christ. Look at the hand of God on your life!

There is too much at stake. You don't need this stumbling block, this trap to be a setback in your life. Look to God for strength and TRUTH! Trust Him with your now and your future! Move forward into the new God has prepared for you! Don't miss out on a new life of joy and victory by looking back and yearning for old experiences.

God is doing a new thing in you! You must recognize it, believe it, and run with it! Be honest with God about your needs, but please do not be deceived! What you left behind is poisonous, and will distract you from your destiny!

DON'T GO BACK!

A Time of Training!

Recognize these thoughts? "I should be further than I am right now. Look at me! Why am I doing this? Why is it hard for me to get ahead? I need to move! I need more in my life! I can do more! I have a college degree, and this job is way below my abilities! I always imagined a better life for myself than this! By this time, I had hoped to be doing- this, & that!"

These kinds of thoughts makes us ungrateful. They blind us to the great things God is doing in the midst of our humble beginnings. The Bible tells us, if we are faithful over little, we will be made ruler over much.

Comparing, mumbling, complaining, can make us bitter, angry, ungrateful, full of regrets, jealous, and covetous. Don't despise the place where you are; instead, be determined to LEARN! God is using where you are right now to develop you, to train you for the places, assignments, He has prepared for you!

Where you are now is building your faith. It is being used to make you teachable, trainable. It is developing your character, maturity, endurance, and strength.

Where you are now is not your end! It is a temporary pit stop along your journey! In the Bible, David, Joseph, Jacob, and many more had humble beginnings before greatness! God is using this to train you, to walk more intimately with Him.

He is showing you how to be faithful unto Him, be thankful, and trust Him, while He is developing your ideas, talents, dreams, and gifts. Therefore, learn all you can where you are right now, and stay thankful! Be encouraged!

You are in a TIME OF TRAINING!

Value God's Word!

The Word of God is alive and is TRUE! It is powerful! It is spirit! It goes far beyond logic and common sense.

The Word of God is Faith! Faith is the language of God. It is important to meditate on the word and speak the word of God over every area of your life. Your mind is renewed when you read and hear the Word of God. Use your faith to come into agreement with it in your spirit.

By reading, praying, worshipping, and fellowshipping with other believers, you will experience growth and see changes in your behavior.

So what am I saying? Know the Word of God! Pray it, speak it, and believe it!

It is life unto you! If you have a hard time understanding the *Bible*, find the translation that is easiest for you to comprehend.

God's Word will change you. It will transform you into the true person you are purposed to be in Him! You will discover your identity in Christ.

Hebrews 4:12 (NIV) says, *"For the word of God is alive and active. Sharper than any double-edged sword, it penetrates even to dividing soul and spirit, joints and marrow; it judges the thoughts and attitudes of the heart."*

VALUE GOD'S WORD!

Did Your Best? Now Rest!

"Is it good enough? What will they think? How come I didn't hear anything? I hope to get some feedback! What if they don't like it? What if I left something out? Forgot something?"

All of these questions flooded my mind and emotions whenever I did something for someone or prepared a project! I wanted to exceed their expectations. However, the fear and anxiety that attacked me stemmed from my fear of rejection.

The fear of maybe getting declined, or not getting a chance for another opportunity was always present. I experienced the fear of failure. There were times, I did not feel knowledgeable or capable in what I presented! This time, I prayed to God for peace, and this is what He said to me:

"Did your best?" I said, "YES!" He said, *"Ok, NOW REST! Put it in My hands. Release it to me and TRUST Me with the outcome!"*

Then His peace surrounded me like a shield. I was able to release the project and the unknown outcome into His Hands! Knowing that in ALL things, God will only do what is BEST for me. He will give me wisdom & humility! He will strengthen me to handle whatever He allows.

Lesson: *"Whatever you do, do it heartily, as to the Lord and not to men..."* Colossians 3:23 (NKJV) First, seek His counsel, do it, and release it back to Him! No more anxiety, worry, fear of failure, or rejection! Remember, because you DID YOUR BEST,

Now you can find your REST, in HIM!

Don't Make It Happen! Just Be!

If you're the driven type, the forward-thinker, the constant planner, the strategist, the persistent and determined one, you have awesome attributes!

However, if they are not submitted unto God those same attributes can rob you of your peace and joy! You will find yourself constantly feeling frustrated and overwhelmed. You have to trust in God's ability to bring His will to fruition in your life, and in divine His timing.

The Bible says in Psalm 127:1 (KJV), *"Except the Lord build the house, they labor in vain!"* Submit your plans and goals to the Lord.
Remember, He is the One who gave you the vision! Don't take on a false burden, believing all of the responsibility rests on

you! You can't do this on your own; it's too big for you!

You have to release your will to God and believe that He will fulfill His purposes concerning you! I remember when I used to work so hard and chant to myself, "You have to make it happen!" Then one day, God had a Pastor who barely knew me, pray for me, and said, *"Darling, you don't have to make it happen! JUST BE!"*

Inside, I was like, "WHAT?! JUST BE?!" That took more faith, than all of my labor in trying to make things happen before God's timing!

Lesson: JUST BE, is saying, because God ordained it, it's already done in the spirit! You are now learning how to trust and obey God daily, allowing Him to order your steps. You are just walking out the vision into manifestation. Have faith that everything God has shown you is already done in the spirit & will come to pass!

DON'T MAKE IT HAPPEN!

Just Be!

Your Gifts & Talents Needs An Outlet!

Work, work, work! Go, go, go! Responsibilities are constantly reminding you of all of the things you HAVE to DO!

You're overwhelmed, stressed out by the routine! Whenever you have time, you're either asleep or in front of the TV!

BALANCE!

God has put gifts and talents in you! All of them need to be discovered, and some of them need to be developed. Your gifts, your talents, your creativity, your energy, and things that makes you smile, needs an outlet. Manage your energy wisely. Make time to explore and do things that interest you.

It is important in life to have this outlet to do different things. It gives you the ability to better manage the things you have to do, with greater ease. When you don't make time to release your creativity- your gifts, energy, and passions get stifled inside of you.

Join activity clubs, get training for the gifts you have, schedule time to do things you enjoy! God gave you those gifts and talents to use for His glory! Don't ignore the unction to draw, to sing, to workout in your sport, to plan events, to write, to dance, to organize, to teach. Whatever gifts you have, pay attention to them and give them an outlet!

Your gifts are purposed to be shared with others!

Glorify God with your gifts!

YOUR GIFTS & TALENTS NEEDS AN OUTLET!

Unexpected Opportunities!

Get ready for unexpected opportunities. I pray your spiritual eyes are open to identify them when they come.

No, things will not be perfectly in order in your life! No, these unexpected opportunities will not be obvious! Your decision will not be an easy one. No, you might not even think you are ready for it! Yet, I pray you are able to identify and grab hold of unexpected opportunities as they come!

Sometimes, when you want something, you put all of your energy into it, and nothing stable manifests from it. So you just put it aside, forget about it, dream about it from time to time, but you've lost hope of it becoming a reality.

Especially now, since so much time has passed! You developed a new routine, and plan for your life that is safe and predictable!

I want to tell you that God knows the plans he has for you! Delayed (though it appears to be) does not mean denied! God hasn't changed his mind! Your life can change in a moment, a day, in a phone call, text, or email! Believe God!

Get your expectations up! Renew your faith! Prepare to grab hold of

UNEXPECTED OPPORTUNITIES.

Peter, Do You Love Me!

Everybody knows about the disciple Peter, who denied Jesus three times when the accusers asked him if he was one of His followers! Yet, this was the same Peter who received the revelation of Jesus as the Christ! The Lord told him that upon that revelation He would use Him to build His church and the gates of hell would not prevail against it!

Peter messed up big time! But God never changed His mind or plans concerning him! Instead, Jesus offered Peter the opportunity to profess his love and commitment to him before others. In John 21:15-22 (NIV), Jesus asked him three times, *"Peter, do you Love Me?"*

Every time Peter answered, "Yes," Jesus gave him the command in John 21:16 (NIV) *"Take care of my sheep."*

Jesus gave Peter the invitation to step into leadership! Peter was given the chance to demonstrate his love by obeying and fulfilling the given command. God wants to use you to take care of His sheep! He wants you to walk in love, be compassionate, serve, care about others, and help when it's possible for you to do so. In your serving others as unto God, you will begin to see people as He sees them. You will become a servant-leader.

Put your name in place of Peter's, and hear the Lord ask you,

"Do You Love Me?"

Remember, when you say, *"Yes, Lord!"* receive his command and take care of His sheep.

The Good Part!

This is a waste of time! What am I doing this for? When you're in a situation that seems pointless, what do you do? Do you vent your frustration and

tell others how horrible it was? Or do you put the negative emotions aside, and try to find the lesson in it?

Always remember, whatever God allows in your life, there is something that can be learned from it, to help you improve your life!

It's like the old saying, *"Eat the meat and spit out the bone!"* In other words, take away the GOOD PART from it! When you find the *good part*, you'll find the lesson. It will be the life point you can use to improve your own actions and behavior in the future.

The next time you're at an event, or with others and it seems like a total waste of time, ask God, *"What should I learn from this?"* and focus on

THE GOOD PART!

Transformation Through Pain

I'm learning this right now, as I make changes to live a healthier lifestyle.

When I do strength exercises to build muscle, my trainer celebrates my pain, and struggle!

However, when I began to struggle, I felt weak, and embarrassed. Then one day, God connected this to how I handled life situations! When things flowed with ease, I felt strong! But when there were challenges, conflict, I felt pain, frustration, and wanted to quit!

However, God revealed to me that it was when I felt the weakest, that I was becoming stronger in Him! Challenges build strength! It builds faith! Understand, with resistance comes pain, and pressure-

PRESS THROUGH IT!

It is in 2Corinthians 12:9 (KJV) where God says, *"My strength is made perfect in weakness."*

When you are weak, call on God, who is your Strength!

Pain is a part of the process of change. The pain of seeing yourself in the same state all the time, is greater than the pain of change! However, going through the pain of change will help continue your transformation in God. Endure! Embrace the process of change because your true identity and purpose in Christ Jesus, is waiting to be revealed.

Get your hopes up! There can be a positive TRANSFORMATION THROUGH PAIN.

Troubled About Many Things!

In Luke 10:38-42 (KJV) is the story of Martha and Mary, two sisters, who were blessed to have Jesus as a guest in their home. Martha was busy with hospitality and serving, while Mary sat at Jesus' feet and heard his word!

Martha, frustrated and overwhelmed with work, said to Jesus, *"Lord, dost thou not care that my sister hath left me to serve alone? Bid her therefore that she help me."* Jesus said, *"Martha, Martha, thou art careful and troubled about many things: But one thing is needful: and Mary hath chosen that good part, which shall not be taken away from her."*

You see, Jesus said, 'one thing is needful,' and that is to spend time with Him and hear His Word!

The cares of this life can make you busy, and over-worked! Sometimes you may feel like Martha, that you don't have the support you need to accomplish all the things that needs to be done! When you find yourself *troubled about many things* do what Mary did, choose the ONE thing that is needful!

Step away from the busyness, and sit at Jesus' feet to hear His voice! Spend time with the Lord. He will calm, help, and comfort you. When you are stressed or frustrated, pause and make a change. Remember, with all that you may have going on, "ONE thing is needful," and that is to get into His presence. Pay attention to the moments when you are

TROUBLED ABOUT MANY THINGS!

It's What's Right with You!

Have you thought about all of the things you have been through, or perhaps are going through? If you've suffered from abuse, or your children's path is different from what you've desired for them, or you've suffered in relationships, dealt with serious health issues, been in prison; the question that plagues your mind is,

"What is wrong with me?

Why isn't my life normal?" Maybe it's because something is wrong with me, that I'm so different! Why do I keep drawing the wrong people into my life? I always seem to draw people who seek ways to use me, and never love me.

I want to tell you! It's NOT what's wrong with you!

IT IS WHAT'S RIGHT WITH YOU!

The more challenges you overcome, the greater your testimony, and the greater the power of God in your life! Your anointing is greater, so you can help others overcome the same challenges!
However, it is necessary that you come out first and experience true victory! God is your healer. He is faithful to guide, and completely restore you!

The enemy hates you because of who you are in God. You are a threat!
Don't compare your life to others!
Christ doesn't love you less than anyone else. God's love for you is unconditional.
No longer entertain that question, "*What is wrong with me?!*"

IT'S WHAT IS RIGHT WITH YOU!

YOU ARE CHOSEN BY GOD!

Be Slow To React!

Be mindful of your emotions and feelings. They can come rushing through you like a flood! Then they make you have to go apologize later,

For the things you said, or for your offensive behavior.

Pray to God for temperance and self-control! I love the scripture in Ecclesiastes 5:2 (NIV), *"Do not be quick with your mouth, do not be hasty in your heart to utter anything before God. God is heaven and you are on earth, so let your words be few."* A similar scripture in James 1:19-27 (KJV) says, *"Let every man be swift to hear, slow to speak, slow to wrath."*

When your emotions start flaring up, immediately pray and call on the name of Jesus! Your cry for help will enable Him to help you control your words, and actions. If possible, find an exit and remove yourself from the situation. Sometimes you can't leave, and you may have to pray fervently for strength to keep yourself quiet.

You represent God, and not yourself. In order to walk in victory, you need to have confidence and total dependence on Him in every area of your life. By faith, know that God is with you! He will help you grow, develop your temperance so you can

BE SLOW TO REACT!

In Christ, You Never Lose!

I didn't deserve to be treated like that! Is that how they talk to me! After all this time in this relationship, believing that there was a mutual respect!?! The horror of being treated with contempt! I had to hold my gut, to not say everything I believed they deserved!

"Hold your peace!" I heard the Lord say to my spirit. *"You will do damage, and sabotage your blessing. Give it to ME. I see it all, and they are not going to get away with it. Trust ME to defend you, and protect you. Trust ME with yourself. You have nothing to prove. Allow ME to intervene."*

LESSON: If people think they are justified in their actions by hurting you, they are delusional! It is a big deception. If God be for you, who can be against you and prosper? Do things God's way. Trust Him when HE tells you to be still.

For the Bible says in Romans 12:19 (KJV), *"Vengeance is mine; I will repay, saith the Lord."*

God will reward you and recompense you far greater than they can ever do for you! He will give you double for your trouble. Pray for those who hurt you and spitefully use you.

Yes it hurts, but keep your focus on God! He's got you covered! As long as you purpose in your heart to please Him, you will NEVER come up short! Isaiah 54:17 (KJV) says, *"No weapon that is formed against thee shall prosper"*

Remember, the weapon will be formed, but it will not accomplish its purpose against you!

IN CHRIST, YOU NEVER LOSE!

Forgiveness & Trust

There is no relationship
without forgiveness.

However, forgiving others is not easy to do. You have to ask God to help you forgive others who have hurt you, the way HE completely forgives you. Pray for mercy, and the ability to impart it freely.

I don't know about you, but I tend to struggle with trust after I forgive others.

In my mind, it's I forgive you BUT,
I don't trust you!

Once trust is broken, it takes a long time, to be restored. Then God showed me something!

LESSON: In a relationship, trust is necessary, but you don't have to trust the person! God wants you and me to trust Him! If you have been hurt a lot, a lack of trust for others can be used in a way to protect yourself from future pain. Trust issues can lead to isolation, withdrawal, and loneliness.

Difficulty trusting others is really FEAR.

The only way to overcome fear is to believe God and Trust in Him to protect you! He will guide you in your relationship with others. If you get hurt, God is able to restore you, and to help you continue loving others. He wants you to enjoy relationships throughout your life. Every relationship requires

FORGIVENESS. In every relationship put your TRUST in God.

Read God's Word

Your *Bible* is your road map throughout life. It is the source you go to, to receive directions on how to get from point A to point B. It teaches you how to transition from one level to the next level.

It is also like a car manual, because it provides instructions for your life.

The *Bible* introduces you to God, to yourself, and to your purpose. It teaches you wisdom and how to navigate through life's tests and storms.

I know there are many ways to get the Word of God. There are audiobooks, television, radio broadcasts, online sermons and inspirational books. However, I want to encourage you to study the Word of God and know the Word intimately for yourself. God will reveal things to you in His Word that will minister to you right where you are.

Studying the *Bible* builds your faith. It allows you to know the benefits of your salvation. You will begin to experience the Power in God's Word, as you meditate on it, pray it, and speak it over every area of your life.

When you meditate on the Word of God in your heart, you will begin to pray in faith, with more confidence in His Word. You will no longer pray emotionally, in anxiety, fear, and doubt.

God's Word strengthens you. It stabilizes and increases your Faith. It is alive and purposed to help you receive all Christ has given you in this life.

Know the *Bible* for yourself.

READ GOD'S WORD.

A Soft Answer

Proverbs 15:1 (KJV) says, *"A soft answer turneth away wrath: but grievous words stir up anger."* When there is a misunderstanding or a hurtful exchange between you and another, there are no limits to the list of harmful words that come to your mind to express how you really feel!

Everyone is offended and the situation has the potential to be destructive. Someone has to see the bigger picture and keep the disagreement from ending in permanent separation. That someone is YOU!

God lives on the inside of you and guides you by His Holy Spirit. He will give you the strength to control your response. If needed, God is able to help to keep silent, or give you a soft answer. Either response will neutralize the situation, and prevent the use of potent, grievous words, that would be like pouring gasoline on a fire.

Pray to God to help you with your words. He will give you the wisdom to deliver

A SOFT ANSWER.

Stay Thankful

1Thessalonians 5:18 (KJV): "In everything give thanks: for this is the will of God in Christ Jesus concerning you."

Have you ever wondered what is the will of God for your life?

Well! It is to give thanks in everything. You know why?

Being thankful helps you become aware of His presence. It helps you be able to see God's Hand consistently at work in your life.

Even in bad situations, you can find something to give God thanks for, because it can always be worse. Thankfulness gives you peace. Giving thanks guards your heart from murmuring and complaining, which leads you to failure and darkness.

Being thankful to God keeps your spirit full of light! It keeps you in a position of humility that allows you to hear, receive, and be led by His instructions.

Being thankful will lead you into God's perfect will for your life!

Thanksgiving keeps you connected to God.

STAY THANKFUL.

Don't Worry

There is a Bob Marley song that says, "Baby don't worry! About a thing! Cause every little thing is gonna be alright!" That is your word today –

DON'T WORRY!

God said in Isaiah 41:10 (NIV), "Do not fear, for I AM with you; do not be dismayed, for I am your God. I will strengthen you and help you; I will uphold you with my righteous right hand."

Have this confidence today, that the LORD is your help! He cannot and will not fail! The LORD has heard your every prayer, knows your every need. He needs your faith to believe in Him, to take care of you, and those you love!

Matthew 6:25 (NIV), tells us, "Do not worry about your life."

Worry and fear brings torment and resolves absolutely nothing! Trust in God. Stand firm on His Word. Your confidence and faith in God will bring you peace in the midst of the storm. Keep Calm and

DON'T WORRY.

Affirmations

Affirmations are declarations, statements.

There is power in your words.

It is important for you to have, or create a list of statements to declare over your life daily. You steer your day, your future, your life, even the lives of others, with your words. Your words are very powerful!

When you speak the Word of God over your life and into the lives of others, it results in transformation. I challenge you to write a list of statements, scriptures, and then say them out loud daily, in faith!

Believe that when your words are in agreement with God's Word there will be manifestation. There will be change because it will come to pass.

If you have areas in your life that are negative, such as believing you are not smart enough or good enough, you must create affirmations that are opposite of the negative things you have believed about yourself or your life.

Declare out loud, in front of a mirror, *"I am smart. I can do all things in Christ.*

God has made me wonderful."
Enjoy creating your affirmations. Place them in areas that are visible to you daily! As you speak them, your actions and attitude will line up with your

AFFIRMATIONS.

Overcome Evil with Good

Romans 12:21 (KJV) says, "Be not overcome by evil, but overcome evil with good." Proverbs 25:21 (NIV) says, "If your enemy is hungry, give him food to eat; if he is thirsty give him water to drink."

The LIFE LESSON God wants us to practice in relationships with others, and even in relationship with ourselves, is to OVERCOME EVIL WITH GOOD.

When people are rude and offensive, don't just ignore them or their offense, but be mindful to remain kind and respectful in your attitude. Negative attitudes are contagious, and if you do not block them with good attitudes, you will become dark too, through offense.

Another example might be, if you decide to stop eating large quantities of junk food to improve your health. You have to replace the junk food with nutritional food, in order to experience the true benefits of changing your diet.

One activity has to be replaced with another activity. You can't just stop something, and not do anything. You have to be consistent in your new activity. If not, you will then lose momentum, and eventually fall back into old habits.

Every action begins with a thought. So when God cleans the rooms in your house, 'your house' being the inner man. Fill those clean rooms with the Word of God. This will help strengthen you when evil is present, and will help you walk in wisdom. When you have filled that area with the things of God, you close the door to the enemy. You see, the enemy thinks that the area where you put him out is still his territory, and will try to come back stronger.

Remember with everything, we must OVERCOME EVIL WITH GOOD.

Give Him You!

What God wants more than anything is not your works or efforts.

God wants YOU!

You are the most valuable gift HE has. God gave you His best, which is Jesus Christ, who paid for your sins to reconcile you back to Himself. Through Christ, He has made it possible for you to enjoy direct fellowship with Him.

God gave you Holiness, Righteousness, Salvation, as gifts for you to receive, so He can enjoy sweet communion with you. God is in love with you!

The relationship between you and God is to overflow with love, mercy, and grace, not with guilt, fear, condemnation, and rejection.

Come to Jesus as you are! You can't change yourself! He is not asking you to, because HE knows you cannot experience true change and freedom without Him!

Know God intimately! Receive His forgiveness for your sins. Forgive yourself. Leave your past in the past, begin to have confidence in His unconditional love for you! God is not looking at your works. God looks at your heart. He knows that if you keep hanging out with Him, His love will transform you, and your actions will change.

God looks at you with a desire to love, heal, and restore you!
Receive His love today.

GIVE HIM YOU.

Emotions

Vashti, a queen in the book of Esther in the Bible, was very beautiful and had a lot of power and influence! Her outcome was not good. However, when you look at the whole story of Esther, you can see how God uses persons and positions to accomplish His purpose.

God used Vashti's behavior to open the door for Esther to become queen, so He can use her to save the Jewish people from destruction. I like Vashti. I can relate to her moods, because I too, have been vulnerable to my emotions!

The story of Vashti helps me remember how much I can lose if I don't bring my emotions under subjection to God! We have to give God our personality and depend on Him to help us control our temperament! In other words, we must bring our flesh, which is our immature

behavior, in line with God's word,
His character, and His way
of doing things.

A little background on Vashti:
There was a banquet she and her husband,
the king had for their royal officials and
other leaders. The king wanted to show off
her beauty to his friends at the banquet,
so he sent for her to come! Perhaps,
Vashti wasn't in the mood to join the king,
so she refused to come. As a result,
she was rejected as queen, was never
permitted to enter the king's presence
again, and lost everything.

LESSON: Following your emotions can
lead you to great lose! When they are
strong, take a deep breath, and consider all
of the consequences before you respond
with your feelings.

Ask God to help you do what is right,
and control your

EMOTIONS.

Courage Is A Gift

Courage enables a person to face difficulty, danger, and pain, without fear. Courage is a demonstration of bravery.

Not everyone has the courage to confront others. This can be due to insecurities, passiveness, or fear.

One day I listened to a Christian talk show, and the host was sharing information on a topic. Then a caller dialed into the show to join the discussion. The caller was hostile, and began to share very disturbing views and opinons. The caller stayed on the line and spoke negative comments for the duration of the broadcast. I couldn't help but ask God, "Why didn't the host address this? Why did they allow the broadcast to get so out of control?"

Then I heard in my spirit, *"COURAGE is a gift!"*

It takes courage to do the right thing.

God uses courage in leadership. Not everyone is courageous. There are some people who are passive, or fear rejection. However, those who possess courage must submit this powerful, influential gift under God. David, a valiant warrior possessed the gift of courage. Before the battle with Golitah, he killed a lion and a

bear with his hands. His confidence in God developed so much privately, that when the opportunity came to confront the dreadful enemy, Goliath, David believed in God to empower him for victory. He was the only one who stepped forward to fight!

David also knew how to submit his gift of courage to God. In 1Samuel 30:8 (KJV) he sought God's counsel on whether to pursue an enemy, asking if he would have victory in that battle. He prayed to God before taking action. God then assured David victory in 1Samuel 30:8 (KJV) and told him to, *"Pursue: for thou shalt surely overtake them, and without fail recover all."*

LESSON: God will always strategically guide us, because our actions impact many. The courageous must seek God first, in all matters. Then step out, and take prompt action on the instructions received.

COURAGE IS A GIFT FROM GOD!

Remove The Mountain

Everything can seem overwhelming.
It can feel like a weight, a pressure that makes your vision blurry!

You don't know where to begin! The thought of quitting brings a feeling of peace- a release from the pressure of this mountain- of things to do!

You have goals, things you know God has put on your heart to do. You have aspirations, dreams, but everything seems so much bigger than you.

Bigger than your abilities! Some of you have made an attempt at it in the past, but you got stuck, never finished, or were not successful. Yet, the desires are still there. Finish it!

See it finished, and ask God to give you the action plan to get it finished.

This mountain is not there to stop you,
but it is there for you to overcome it!
Don't let fear grip your heart when you
look at that mountain. On the other side of
it is your promise.

Take a good look at that mountain!
Don't let it overwhelm you! Don't Quit!

Set your own pace and keep pressing
forward! Mark 11:23 (KJV) says,
*"For verily I say unto you,
That whosoever shall say unto this
mountain, Be thou removed, and be thou
cast into the sea; and shall not doubt in his
heart, but shall believe that those things
which he saith shall come to pass;
he shall have whatsoever he saith."*

In Christ, you can conquer and

REMOVE THAT MOUNTAIN!

It's Personal!

God of the universe, over all the earth, is personally, intimately involved with you! The Bible says in Luke 12:7 (NIV), He even knows the number of hairs on your head! God is completely in tuned with you!

With all that is going on in the world, God gives attention to your every prayer. There is no prayer too small. God wants to be involved in every area of your life. The blessings God gives you daily are personal!

I want to open up your awareness to the way He answers prayers never uttered. God perceives your needs and heart desires, down to the detail of finding your favorite movie on television, or a much needed parking space.

I want you to be aware of the many ways God expresses His personal love to you each day!

Thankfulness helps us to recognize His consistent random acts of kindness!
The more you become aware of God's personal love towards you, your praise and thanksgiving will automatically increase.

God's love towards you is unconditional!

The daily blessings He purposely bestows upon you are well thought out!

IT'S PERSONAL!

Use The Name!

Spoiler Alert! I saw the movie *'Creed'* with Sylvester Stallone. I'm going to tell you the part of the movie that ministered to me.

There are quite a number of Rocky sequels. However, in this movie, Rocky decides to train Apollo Creed's son as a professional boxer. They get an opportunity to fight an undefeated champion of the world. However, in order to seize this offer, Rocky's prodigy has to use his father's name "CREED!"

In the movie, the name Creed represented a legacy of excellence, talent, power, and strength! It put more pressure on him because he had to believe within himself that he could fulfill the expectations attached to that name!

The young prodigy waivered with embracing his father's name!

His girlfriend said to him, *"Focus on what is true. Are you Apollo's son?"* He said, *"Yes."* Then she said, *"Use the Name!"*
I want you to know this Truth! In Christ, you are sons and daughters of the most High God! You are the one to continue the legacy of love, kindness, strength, victory, and power! In Jesus, you share in His righteousness, His holiness, His wisdom, His power. Through Him, you can enjoy a direct relationship with God our Father.

In this life, you don't have to stand alone and try to make it on your own merit! Jesus is the name above all names!

You are chosen. You belong to Him, and in Him you have value. You are royalty. You are righteous. You have love! You have the power to bring change through JESUS CHRIST!

USE **HIS** NAME!

The Spirit Check!

Pride and haughtiness are not of God.

They are sneaky, and try to manifest in our thoughts, in how we look at others who are different from us. It is a deception.

Jesus never scorned or mistreated anyone. He was open to all people and gave them the attention many others would not. The lame, orphans, widows, the barren, the adulterer, the people who were hard to love, the ones who seem way too far gone to change, all were valuable to Him.

He sat and communed with people who were scorned and discarded by society. Jesus experienced rejection by others, because of His outreach to the sick and the lost.

If you ever feel the temptation within yourself to scorn, mistreat, or put down someone, check that feeling immediately! It is not from God, so don't let it linger.

It is a deception that will blind you and keep you from

Walking in love and serving others, as Christ did in the earth.

Pride will consume your inner being like a poison, and change your whole countenance from kind, to selfish and mean-spirited.

So when your feelings tempt you to be rude, critical, judgmental, and harsh towards others,

DO THE SPIRIT CHECK! Check that attitude, pray immediately, and replace it with positive words or the Word of God. This will keep you out of darkness and allow you to dwell in the LIGHT and personality of Jesus Christ!

Release The Grip!

The fear of losing something dear to you makes you want to hang on tightly and try to preserve it with your own strength!

It can be your spouse, children, a job, or material things.

Sometimes you may compromise your standards, take more abuse, or experience anxiety attacks because you are afraid of living life without that person, job position or tangible thing.

Whatever you hang on to too tightly, will wither and die.

RELEASE THE GRIP.

It is not your job to preserve it, or worry about it. God wants you to release the person, job, or material possession to His care!

It is God's will for you to find rest in your soul, your mind, and your emotions by trusting in Him. You have to believe God's Word and His promises towards you.

If anything comes to an end, trust God's omnipotence and timing. Believe that if HE allowed it to be removed,
He will carry you through it with grace and victory.

God will lead you and heal you, in your transition. He will also comfort you as you experience grief from the loss.

Always know that God has only good in store for you. He is always leading you to better. You can trust Him with Everything!

Don't hang onto anyone or anything to the point, where you're afraid to lose it.

Only cleave to God! Everything else is temporary. RELEASE THE GRIP!

Intentionally Cruel

I have learned that when persons are intentionally cruel and reject you,

They behave this way to protect THEMSELVES.

The insensitive, spiteful persons are full of fear, anger, and pain. They are putting up a front, a diversion to hide the pain they feel inside. Some may call it "blowing smoke," which is trying to get you to focus on the drama and not see the real truth about the matter, or the real truth about them.

A lot of times, they act like this to try to avenge themselves from a previous offense, or try to get the upper hand in the relationship. In other words, they hurt you before you can hurt them, or they try to hurt you more than you have hurt them.

Their actions cause pain, confusion, rejection, and anxiety to others. You may wonder why they said a particular thing.

You ask, *"Why are they acting like this?! Why did they do that? What did I do?"*

Honestly, don't take it personally! The real problem is the war that is happening on the inside of them. You just got caught up in the crossfire. To protect their vulnerability, they attack what's closest to them – You! Again, Don't take it personally. It's really not about you!

Ask God to heal your broken heart from the offense and the pain! Don't be afraid to be still, and rest in God. He will give you the wisdom, courage and self-love to be able to move on to more wholesome connections, as you recover from the blows to your emotions. You will heal. You will grow. You will get stronger. You will become wiser. You will be able to separate yourself from them enough, to pray with a pure a heart of compassion for those who are INTENTIONALLY CRUEL.

Validation

Whenever you need validation from any source other than God, you become vulnerable to deception.

If you constantly have to be affirmed or validated by those whom you admire, you will be misused.

You will be emotionally unstable. You will be tossed like the wind by others' ever-changing opinions of you. There are people who prey upon and manipulate those who don't know who they are. God wants you to know that you are valuable!

You don't have to try to get the approval from those you esteem! You do not need their approval to define you, make you feel needed, or believe you are somebody special!

Let me tell you about a hoax I almost fell for, and how God revealed this lesson to me! A very notable, renowned preacher contacted me via social media. I wondered to myself, *"With all of their thousands of followers, why would they reach out to me? Did my post bless them? What's going on?"* Then, I got all excited, jumped up & down, felt overjoyed, I mean really, oh my gosh! They contacted ME?! They sent me a prayer, and after several messages a request for money. At that point, I went to the website of the famous preacher. On their web page it said, they do not ask for money via emails, messages, or by phone. It was then I realized this was a hoax, a scam!

Thankfully, I did not fall for the scam. Yet the highs, the lows of emotions and even shame for almost being deceived, plagued me all at once. Why did I get so excited? If it were the real renowned preacher, would it have confirmed within me, or to others that I was special?

When you are needy for love and have low self-esteem, you either subject yourself to others who may take advantage of you, OR you use others notoriety to make yourself feel like you're somebody! Believe God's Word, and receive His love for you! LOVE YOURSELF! You Are Somebody in HIM! Receive God's

VALIDATION.

Freedom Has A Purpose

FREE. What does that word mean to you? When most people hear the word "Free" they light up! It can be a free gift, or the permission to be free to make your own decisions! Free is connected to the word Freedom! FREEDOM brings joy!

It is through Christ that a person can experience TRUE Freedom!

However, with liberty there is also responsibility!

We all have a responsibility to make sure our actions are not oppressing the freedom of others.

When Jesus paid for our sins on the cross, He gave us liberty, or freedom from religion, hate, anger, emotional, physical sickness, addictions, and so much more!

We receive true freedom in Christ by faith! We receive grace and mercy daily for our mistakes.

However, with our freedom we must try not hurt people with our words, or mislead others by engaging in actions that may be harmful to those with weaker faith.
We must be mindful of those who do not yet know the love, grace, or mercy of God.

LESSON: Let us submit our Freedom to God and His way of doing things.
Yes, we may be free to do this and that, but let's be careful with our actions as ambassadors of Christ. Freedom is not to be abused. It should be used to build up the lives of others.

FREEDOM HAS A PURPOSE.

God Promotes!

I confess! I got out of hand! The things I used to thank God for, I began to take for granted. I developed an attitude of entitlement and saw my blessings as a RIGHT versus a PRIVILEGE!

For example, I've been at my job for a long time. In the beginning, I was praising God for it! Then time passed, and I felt, *"Hey, where's my raise? I should be promoted by now! I'm sick of this! The people here are this &that! I don't want to do this anymore!"*

My attitude changed from positive to negative, to bitter, and to entitled! I walked around like somebody owed me something! Hey, I was good at what I did (by God's grace of course) but by this time humility was out the window! I wanted to be properly compensated for the success I was helping the company to achieve.

LESSON: Promotion doesn't come from man! Promotion comes from the Lord! (Psalm 75:6 KJV) God had to remind me that there were plenty of people who would love to have the position I was griping about! He showed me that I was not trusting in Him, but was depending on outside circumstances, people, and their actions to validate me and make me happy.

I had to make a serious attitude adjustment from pride and entitlement to THANKSGIVING! I had to humble myself and trust God and His timing!

Promotion came eventually, but only after I changed my attitude.

Take everything to God in prayer. Always find a way to stay Thankful in situations! Thanksgiving keeps you on a path to experience God's best for your life. **GOD PROMOTES!**

Action Needed

There is power in unity. If you are really passionate about a cause, get involved! Your participation makes a difference!

I know you can look at the people gathered and say to yourself, *"Well, they have enough people, they will be fine."* However, no one can replace your presence or share what you have to offer!

Find ways to get involved that will fit your lifestyle. If you can offer time, share your time. If you can offer money, donate money. Anything you give to help, whether it is big or small, will always be an increase, a gain, and never a loss!

Your contribution matters. Commit yourself to the cause God has put on your heart. What are you passionate about? Ask God to show you how you can serve those who need your help.

You have something to offer!
Serving others with a pure heart
and genuine, sincere motives brings
inner fulfillment.

Get involved!

YOUR ACTION IS NEEDED!

On Your Mind

It's funny at times how a person will randomly keep coming to your mind. You may say to yourself, *"Oh, I wonder how they are doing?"* Or you may recall an event or memory when you last spoke to each other.

Sometimes you can be in the car or a store, and a song comes on that reminds you of them! Pay attention to those repetitive thoughts about those persons.

Sometimes they may reach out to you first, because you were on their mind too!

When God puts someone on your heart, don't take it lightly. It's not a

coincidence! It is a moment to pause and ask God why that person is on your mind. Then you should say a prayer for them.

There is no distance in prayer.
There are no limits in the spirit!

God uses our prayers to meet the needs of others.

God doesn't make mistakes.
When He puts someone on your heart,

He chose YOU to reach out to them, pray, or do both!

That is why they are

ON YOUR MIND!

Keep Your Eyes On Him

Are you afraid of success? Sounds like a silly question, doesn't it?

Who would be afraid of success? Isn't that what most people want?

The stress, the attention, the responsibilities may be seen as a deterrent, rather than an exciting push forward into new opportunities.

Fear of success occurs when the focus on the negative, outweighs its positive benefits.

Please do not allow fear to rule your life. Do not let fear keep you from the plans God has already established for you!

Fear paralyzes you, and will make you afraid to move forward. If you fear success, you may have a personal struggle with trusting God.

Fear, or a lack of trust in God, will cause you walk in disobedience. You will avoid the direction God is leading you. You will stay complacent and never become all that you were created to be. Don't be afraid of success, because of pride, failure, and the many negative attributes that can come with it.

Keep your eyes on God. If you stay close to Him on the journey, you will remain humble. You will always remember that it was the Lord who made everything possible. You will honor Him before others, by giving Him the glory for everything they admire about your life.

God has nothing but good in store for you! He says in Jeremiah 29:11 (NIV) He has, *"...plans to prosper you, not to harm you."* God is able to keep you in the midst of success. I've heard someone say, "If He brings you to it, He will see you through it!" Move forward. Trust God.

KEEP YOUR EYES ON HIM

Building Blocks

The activities God is leading you to do in this season are like building blocks.

Piece by piece, brick by brick, you are strategically drawing closer to fulfilling your purpose, one brick at a time.

You see, God has given you a vision and now it is time for it to spring forth! Behold, God is doing a new thing! *"Shall ye not know it..."* Isaiah 43:19 (KJV)

Everything in the kingdom of God is about timing. It is a cycle of sowing and reaping. It requires seed, time, and harvest. The Bible mentions in 1 Corinthians 3:6-8 (NKJV), One plants, one waters, but only God brings the increase.

Every act of obedience is leading you to more divine connections, greater ideas, and more knowledge. Obedience to God will allow you to experience more increase in your life!

Brick by brick, piece by piece, the puzzle will become clearer as you obey God promptly. God has given you the vision, but He may not tell you every step, or reveal all of the details. The just shall live by faith. Faith is believing God at His word before you see any supporting detail manifest in your life.

As you move forward in God by faith, more answers will be revealed.

In building, it is important to make sure your foundation is firm with prompt obedience, faith, and patience. Don't get anxious and overwhelmed. Pray for wisdom and supernatural peace in your spiritual construction site!

The vision will come to pass. Trust & Obey God as He shows you how to correctly place the

BUILDING BLOCKS.

Conclusion

There will be things that happen in your life that you will not understand.

You may ask God why, and may not get an answer. However, you will have to come to a conclusion on what you believe about God.

Do you believe that He loves you, is able to take care of you, and will see you through?

Or do you believe that He has abandoned you, and this should not have happened to you?

It is easy to be offended and disappointed at God when things happen in your life that are difficult to understand.

The Bible shares that God is full of mercy and grace, and that He's a healer, a comforter, a deliverer!

It is only with your faith, you can please God and have a wonderful relationship with Him. Faith doesn't have to understand God. Faith is the ability to trust God!

Examine your heart. Don't be deceived and believe negative things about God, based on logic and one-sided observations. Why separate yourself from the only ONE who can help you and bring good changes to your life?

Life isn't fair, and every bit of news received will not always be good. However, believe that God is for you and not against you.

Those who decide to believe and trust in Him, regardless of circumstances, will be able to overcome and navigate through this life victoriously.

You Are Needed

It is important to make sure insecurities and feelings of low self esteem are conquered in the name of Jesus!

They are stumbling blocks and breeding grounds for envy, competition, and covetousness.

God desires to heal you, so your relationship with Him and with others will be whole. It is a process. God will reveal the origin of pain in your life, layer by layer. Be assured that He will continue and complete the work He has begun in you!

God's command is to love Him, yourself and others. We are commanded to love in that exact order. However, the toxic emotions from insecurity and low self-esteem will cause havoc in every relationship in your life.

When God heals you, you are free to love! You will no longer use your energy to try to be loved by people.

You will then be able to identify the same pain in others and help them overcome too. The love that flows from you may be the only God-like love a person may ever experience. It will cause them to want more of God, and stir up a hunger and thirst for Him.

It is God's will to use you as the bridge to reconcile Him to His people.

No longer tolerate feelings of low self-esteem and insecurity!

There are too many people who are hurting, that need help.

YOU ARE NEEDED

Learn From Feedback

Guard your ideas. Share them with people whose opinions you respect.

Train your ear to hear wisdom.

Whether they are excited about your idea, or find it questionable, let your guard down and listen carefully.

Don't be overly sensitive, and resist the temptation to take offense. Try to make the conversation atmosphere open, so they will be comfortable being honest with you.

Ask questions. Listen for the good and bad points about your idea. Ask for suggestions on how to improve it, if they were not offered. If you get a negative response, calm down and try to listen objectively to their reasoning. If you get a positive response, listen for ways to take the idea to the next level.

Whatever the outcome, if you really believe in the idea, pursue it!

In the end, you will be accountable for your decisions concerning that vision.

Seeking counsel for your ideas is very wise. Use feedback as a step to go higher. Do not let opposing opinions shut you down. Continue to build, and be flexible to make adjustments. Grab hold of the useful information provided, and discard whatever isn't necessary.

As the old saying goes, *"Eat the meat and spit out the bones!"*

LEARN FROM FEEDBACK

Just Ask

I found myself fretting over a new project.

I began thinking about all of the things I didn't know, and even considered the option to quit, even though I knew it was a task God wanted me to do.

What was once exciting became more and more scary as I learned about the necessary details.

One day, I was talking with my Mom and she said to me, *"Why don't you ask God to help you, and make everything flow with ease?"*

Simple prayer! Why didn't I think of that?! Then she said to me, *"The problem is that you don't ask!"*

For many of us, this is true. We take on the burden and stress of a situation and OWN it! We carry the weight on our shoulders, many times not even sharing it with others who can possibly help us!

Do you ask God for help and release it to Him by faith?

Sometimes I pray for help, and then later I beat my brain trying to figure things out!

LESSON: There is a simple way to receive help! Matthew 7:7 (KJV) says, *"Ask, and it will be given you; seek and ye shall find; knock, and it shall be opened unto you."* Practice dependency on God. Remember that He is a very present help! God wants us to believe He is able to make the difference when we seek Him and

JUST ASK.

Rest

Time goes by so fast! Go-go-go!

You hustle to make the money, pay the bills, support the family, and maintain relationships. In this vicious cycle you can become rigid, and oblivious to your need to REST.

It becomes difficult to calm the brain, calm your spirit, and turn off the "ON" button! Even when you go on vacation, you're on the go! You end up needing a vacation from the vacation!

When you are calm, ideas, and thoughts become more clear. It is not God's will for you to run at full speed all of the time! Even machines need to shut down to rest or receive download.

God granted Himself a Sabbath day after creating the world, demonstrating to us the importance of rest.

All work and no play isn't living! God wants you to enjoy the journey! Ecclesiastes 3:13 (NKJV) says, *"...Every man should eat and drink and enjoy the good of all his labor—it is the gift of God."* Put GOD first! Cast your cares on Him, and find enjoyable ways to de-stress.

Rearrange your schedule. Reprioritize your life. Be determined to make time to

REST!

You Are A Champion

Look how far you've come! Look how far the Lord has brought you!

You may not be where you want to be, but you are not where you used to be!

You are TRIUMPHANT!

You are an overcomer! The Hand of the Lord is upon you!

You are the apple of God's eye!

God will fulfill His purposes concerning you! Don't be discouraged at the obstacles and challenges when they arise!

You will use them as stepping stones to climb higher and reach new heights.

You are POWERFUL!

"Greater is HE that is in you, than he that is in the world." 1John 4:4 (KJV)

God will never leave you. He will never abandon you!

Psalm 34:19 (NKJV) says, *"Many are the afflictions of the righteous, but the LORD delivers him out of them all."*

The Lord is your protector, your strong tower, your safety, your deliverer!

You can persevere in faith!

You can move forward because

YOU ARE A CHAMPION!

Contact Ayana Bernard at:

YanniAyana1@gmail.com

www.YanniAyana.com

www.ingramcontent.com/pod-product-compliance
Lightning Source LLC
Chambersburg PA
CBHW072055290426
44110CB00014B/1688